The Regius Poem
or
Halliwell Manuscript

By

King Solomon

Copyright © 2020 Lamp of Trismegistus. All rights reserved. No part of this publication may be reproduced or transmitted in any form or by any means, electronic or mechanical, including photocopying, recording, or by any information storage and retrieval system, without permission in writing from Lamp of Trismegistus. Reviewers may quote brief passages.

ISBN: 978-1-63118-447-5

Foundations of Freemasonry Series

Other Books in this Series and Related Titles

The Mysteries of Freemasonry & the Druids
by Albert G. Mackey, Manly P. Hall &c (978-1-63118-444-4)

A Few Masonic Sermons
by A. C. Ward & Bascom B. Clarke (978-1-63118-435-2)

Royal Arch, Capitular and Cryptic Masonry
by various authors (978-1-63118-425-3)

Masonic Symbolism of King Solomon's Temple
by Albert G. Mackey &c (978-1-63118-442-0)

Psalms of Solomon by King Solomon (978-1-63118-439-0)

The Lost Keys of Freemasonry or The Secret of Hiram Abiff
by Manly P. Hall (978-1-63118-427-7)

The Two Great Pillars of Boaz and Jachin
by Albert G. Mackey, H. L. Haywood, William Harvey & others
(978-1-63118-433-8)

Ancient Egyptian Mysteries and Hieroglyphics, Modern Freemasonry & Initiation of the Pyramid by various authors (978-1-63118-430-7)

Masonic Symbolism of Easter and the Christ in Masonry
by various authors (978-1-63118-434-5)

Symbolism and Discourses on the Entered Apprentice, Fellowcraft and Master Mason Blue Lodge Degrees by various (978-1-63118-413-0)

Masonic Symbolism of the Apron & the Altar
by various authors (978-1-63118-428-4)

The Story and Legend of Hiram Abiff by William Harvey, Manly P. Hall & Albert G. Mackey (978-1-63118-411-6)

Audio Versions are also Available on Audible and iTunes

Table of Contents

Introduction...7

Prologue...9

Here begin the constitutions of the art of Geometry according to Euclid...13

Here begins the first article...17

Second article...19

Third article...21

Fourth article...23

Fifth article...25

Sixth article...27

Seventh article...29

Eighth article...31

Ninth article...33

Tenth article...35

Eleventh article...37

Twelfth article...39

Thirteenth article...41

Fourteenth article...43

Fifteenth article...45

Plural constitutions

First point...47

Second point...49

Third point...51

Fourth point...53

Fifth point...55

Sixth point...57

Seventh point...59

Eighth point...61

Ninth point...63

Tenth point...65

Eleventh point...67

Twelfth point...69

Thirteenth point...71

Fourteenth point...73

Fifteenth point...75

Another ordinance of the art of geometry...77

The art of the four crowned ones...79

Introduction

From the beginning of Modern Freemasonry's birthdate of 1717, the intelligentsia of humanity have found refuge for safe reflection within the walls of the fraternity. Masonic writers have produced a nearly incalculable amount of written musings on a multitude of esoteric and philosophical subjects, as they relate to the ancient mysteries that Freemasonry currently storehouses. Sadly, most of it appears to have sat largely unread, as American Freemasonry in particular, continues to transform itself into something that bears little resemblance to what it was originally designed to be. The true essence of Freemasonry is not that of blind patriotism or a single-minded national religion but one of Universal Brotherhood and altruism, designed for the betterment not just of its members but of society as a whole. In particular, for those who are not members of the fraternity, as Freemasonry has always acted as a beacon, to help guide humanity through darker times, with the hopes that one day we will collectively reach a truly enlightened age.

It's not uncommon for new members joining the fraternity to find little education within the walls of many modern lodges, in spite of so much written material available to the membership. Many older members are not simply uneducated with regards to real Masonic history and symbology, not to mention the vast arena of related subjects, but they are disinterested in all of it, as well.

Lamp of Trismegistus is doing its part to help preserve humanity's Masonic history by making some of these classics available to those students who are seeking to unearth the knowledge of these ancient colossi. As such, Lamp of Trismegistus offers its readers highlights of Masonic study, culled from a variety of authors and viewpoints, with the hope bringing education back into the fraternity. So, be sure to check out other titles in our *Foundations of Freemasonry Series* as well as our *Esoteric Classics, Theosophical Classics, Occult Fiction* and our *Christian Apocrypha Series*, and don't be afraid to let a little altruism into your own heart or even into your Lodge. You can also download the audio versions of most of these titles from iTunes or Audible, for learning on the go.

Prologue

The *Old Charges* of the masons' lodges were documents describing the duties of the members, part of which (*the charges*) every mason had to swear to, on admission. For this reason, every lodge had a copy of the charges, occasionally written into the beginning of the minute book, but usually as a separate manuscript roll of parchment. With the introduction of Grand Lodges, these were largely superseded by printed constitutions, but the Grand Lodge of All England at York, and the few lodges that remained independent in Scotland and Ireland, retained the hand-written charges as their authority to meet as a lodge. Woodford, Hughan, Speth and Gould, all founders of Quatuor Coronati Lodge, and Dr Begemann, a German Freemason, produced much published work in the second half of the nineteenth century, collating, cataloguing, and classifying the available material. Since then, aside from the occasional rediscovery of another old document, little has been done to update the field.

The oldest, the *Regius Poem*, is unique in being set in verse. The rest, of which over a hundred survive, usually have a three-part construction. They start with a prayer, invocation of God, or a general declaration, followed by a description of the Seven Liberal Arts (logic, grammar, rhetoric, arithmetic, geometry, music and astronomy), extolling Geometry above the others. There follows a history of the craft, and how it came to the British Isles, usually culminating in a general assembly of masons during the reign of King Athelstan. The last part consists of the charges or regulations of the lodge, and the craft of masonry in general, which the members are bound to maintain.

The *Regius Poem*, also known as the *Halliwell Manuscript*, is the earliest of the Old Charges. It consists of 64 vellum pages of Middle English written in rhyming couplets. In this, it differs from the prose of all the later charges. The poem begins by describing how Euclid "counterfeited geometry" and called it masonry, for the employment of the children of the nobility in Ancient Egypt. It then recounts the spread of the art of geometry in "divers lands." The document relates how the craft of masonry was brought to England during the reign of King Athelstan (924–939). It tells how all the masons of the land came to the King for direction as to their own good governance, and how Athelstan, together with the nobility and landed gentry, forged the fifteen articles and fifteen points for their rule. This is followed by the aforementioned fifteen articles for the master, concerning both moral behavior (do not harbor thieves, do not take bribes, attend church regularly, etc.) and the operation of work on a building site (do not make your masons labor at night, teach apprentices properly, do not take on jobs that you cannot do etc.). There are then fifteen points for craftsmen which follow a similar pattern. Warnings of punishment for those breaking the ordinances are followed by provision for annual assemblies. There follows the legend of the Four Crowned Martyrs, a series of moral aphorisms, and finally a blessing.

"Fyftene artyculus þey þer sow3ton, and fyftene poyntys þer þey wro3ton." (Fifteen articles they there sought and fifteen points there they wrought.) —Regius MS, ca. 1425-50.

The origins of the Regius are obscure. The manuscript was recorded in various personal inventories as it changed hands until it came into possession of the Royal Library, which was donated to the British Museum in 1757 by King George II, to form the nucleus of the present British Library. It came to the attention of Freemasonry much later, this oversight being mainly due to the librarian David Casley, who described it as "a Poem of Moral Duties" when he catalogued it in 1734. It was in the 1838–39 session of the Royal Society that James Halliwell, who was not a Freemason, delivered a paper on "The early History of Freemasonry in England", based on the Regius, which was published in 1840. The manuscript was dated to 1390, and supported by such authorities as Woodford and Hughan, the dating of Edward Augustus Bond, the curator of manuscripts at the British Museum, to fifty years later was largely sidelined. Hughan also mentions that it was probably written by a priest. *Here we have attributed the otherwise anonymous poem to King Solomon, out of an oral and historical tradition, only.*

The Regius Poem
Or
Halliwell Manuscript

Here begin the constitutions of the art of Geometry according to Euclid

Whoever will both well read and look
He may find written in old book
Of great lords and also ladies,
That had many children together, certainly;
And had no income to keep them with,
Neither in town nor field nor enclosed wood;
A council together they could them take,
To ordain for these children's sake,
How they might best lead their life
Without great disease, care and strife;
And most for the multitude that was coming
Of their children after great clerks,
To teach them then good works;

And pray we them, for our Lord's sake.
To our children some work to make,
That they might get their living thereby,
Both well and honestly full securely.
In that time, through good geometry,
This honest craft of good masonry
Was ordained and made in this manner,

Counterfeited of these clerks together;
At these lord's prayers they counterfeited geometry,
And gave it the name of masonry,
For the most honest craft of all.
These lords' children thereto did fall,
To learn of him the craft of geometry,
The which he made full curiously;

Through fathers' prayers and mothers' also,
This honest craft he put them to.
He learned best, and was of honesty,
And passed his fellows in curiosity,
If in that craft he did him pass,
He should have more worship than the less,
This great clerk's name was Euclid,
His name it spread full wonder wide.
Yet this great clerk ordained he
To him that was higher in this degree,
That he should teach the simplest of wit
In that honest craft to be perfect;
And so each one shall teach the other,
And love together as sister and brother.

Furthermore yet that ordained he,
Master called so should he be;
So that he were most worshiped,
Then should he be so called;
But masons should never one another call,
Within the craft amongst them all,
Neither subject nor servant, my dear brother,

Though he be not so perfect as is another;
Each shall call other fellows by friendship,
Because they come of ladies' birth.
On this manner, through good wit of geometry,
Began first the craft of masonry;
The clerk Euclid on this wise it found,
This craft of geometry in Egypt land.

In Egypt he taught it full wide,
In divers lands on every side;
Many years afterwards, I understand,
Ere that the craft came into this land.
This craft came into England, as I you say,
In time of good King Athelstan's day;
He made then both hall and even bower,
And high temples of great honour,
To disport him in both day and night,
And to worship his God with all his might.
This good lord loved this craft full well,
And purposed to strengthen it every part,
For divers faults that in the craft he found;
He sent about into the land

After all the masons of the craft,
To come to him full even straight,
For to amend these defaults all
By good counsel, if it might fall.
An assembly then could let make
Of divers lords in their state,
Dukes, earls, and barons also,

Knights, squires and many more,
And the great burgesses of that city,
They were there all in their degree;
There were there each one always,
To ordain for these masons' estate,
There they sought by their wit,
How they might govern it;

Fifteen articles they there sought,
And fifteen points there they wrought,

Here begins the first article

The first article of this geometry:
The master mason must be full securely
Both steadfast, trusty and true,
It shall him never then rue;
And pay thy fellows after the cost,
As victuals goeth then, well thou knowest;
And pay them truly, upon thy faith,
What they may deserve;
And to their hire take no more,
But what that they may serve for;
And spare neither for love nor dread,

Of neither parties to take no bribe;
Of lord nor fellow, whoever he be,
Of them thou take no manner of fee;
And as a judge stand upright,
And then thou dost to both good right;
And truly do this wheresoever thou goest,
Thy worship, thy profit, it shall be most.

Second article

The second article of good masonry,
As you must it here hear specially,
That every master, that is a mason,
Must be at the general congregation,
So that he it reasonably be told
Where that the assembly shall be held;

And to that assembly he must needs go,
Unless he have a reasonable excuse,
Or unless he be disobedient to that craft
Or with falsehood is overtaken,
Or else sickness hath him so strong,
That he may not come them among;
That is an excuse good and able,
To that assembly without fable.

Third Article

The third article forsooth it is,
That the master takes to no 'prentice,
Unless he have good assurance to dwell
Seven years with him, as I you tell,
His craft to learn, that is profitable;

Within less he may no be able
To lords' profit, nor to his own
As you may know by good reason.

Fourth article

The fourth article this must be,
That the master him well be see,
That he no bondman 'prentice make,
Nor for no covetousness do him take;
For the lord that he is bound to,
May fetch the 'prentice wheresoever he go.
If in the lodge he were taken,
Much disease it might there make,
And such case it might befall,
That it might grieve some or all.

For all the masons that be there
Will stand together all together.
If such one in that craft should dwell,
Of divers disease you might tell;
For more ease then, and of honesty,
Take a 'prentice of higher degree.
By old time written I find
That the 'prentice should be of gentle kind;
And so sometime, great lords' blood
Took this geometry that is full good.

Fifth article

The fifth article is very good,
So that the 'prentice be of lawful blood;
The master shall not, for no advantage,

Make no 'prentice that is deformed;
It is mean, as you may hear
That he have all his limbs whole all together;
To the craft it were great shame,
To make a halt man and a lame,
For an imperfect man of such blood
Should do the craft but little good.
Thus you may know every one,
The craft would have a mighty man;
A maimed man he hath no might,
You must it know long ere night.

Sixth article

The sixth article you must not miss

That the master do the lord no prejudice,
To take the lord for his 'prentice,
As much as his fellows do, in all wise.
For in that craft they be full perfect,
So is not he, you must see it.
Also it were against good reason,
To take his hire as his fellows do.

This same article in this case,
Judgeth his prentice to take less
Than his fellows, that be full perfect.
In divers matters, know requite it,
The master may his 'prentice so inform,
That his hire may increase full soon,
And ere his term come to an end,
His hire may full well amend.

Seventh article

The seventh article that is now here,
Full well will tell you all together,
That no master for favour nor dread,
Shall no thief neither clothe nor feed.
Thieves he shall harbour never one,
Nor him that hath killed a man,
Nor the same that hath a feeble name,
Lest it would turn the craft to shame.

Eighth article

The eighth article sheweth you so,
That the master may it well do.
If that he have any man of craft,
And he be not so perfect as he ought,
He may him change soon anon,
And take for him a more perfect man.
Such a man through recklessness,
Might do the craft scant worship.

Ninth article

The ninth article sheweth full well,
That the master be both wise and strong;
That he no work undertake,
Unless he can both it end and make;
And that it be to the lords' profit also,
And to his craft, wheresoever he go;
And that the ground be well taken,
That it neither flaw nor crack.

Tenth article

The tenth article is for to know,
Among the craft, to high and low,
There shall no master supplant another,
But be together as sister and brother,
In this curious craft, all and some,
That belongeth to a master mason.
Nor shall he supplant no other man,
That hath taken a work him upon,
In pain thereof that is so strong,

That weigheth no less than ten pounds,
but if that he be guilty found,
That took first the work on hand;
For no man in masonry
Shall not supplant other securely,
But if that it be so wrought,
That in turn the work to nought;
Then may a mason that work crave,
To the lords' profit for it to save
In such a case if it do fall,
There shall no mason meddle withal.
Forsooth he that beginneth the ground,
If he be a mason good and sound,
He hath it securely in his mind

To bring the work to full good end.

Eleventh article

The eleventh article I tell thee,
That he is both fair and free;
For he teacheth, by his might,
That no mason should work by night,
But if be in practicing of wit,
If that I could amend it.

Twelfth article

The twelfth article is of high honesty
To every mason wheresoever he be,
He shall not his fellows' work deprave,
If that he will his honesty save;
With honest words he it commend,

By the wit God did thee send;
But it amend by all that thou may,
Between you both without doubt.

Thirteenth article

The thirteenth article, so God me save,
Is if that the master a 'prentice have,
Entirely then that he him tell,
That he the craft ably may know,
Wheresoever he go under the sun.

Fourteenth article

The fourteenth article by good reason,
Sheweth the master how he shall do;
He shall no 'prentice to him take,
Unless diver cares he have to make,
That he may within his term,
Of him divers points may learn.

Fifteenth article

The fifteenth article maketh an end,
For to the master he is a friend;
To teach him so, that for no man,
No false maintenance he take him upon,
Nor maintain his fellows in their sin,
For no good that he might win;
Nor no false oath suffer him to make,
For dread of their souls' sake,
Lest it would turn the craft to shame,
And himself to very much blame.

Plural Constitutions

First point

At this assembly were points ordained more,
Of great lords and masters also.
That who will know this craft and come to estate,
He must love well God and holy church always,
And his master also that he is with,
Wheresoever he go in field or enclosed wood,
And thy fellows thou love also,
For that thy craft will that thou do.

Second point

The second point as I you say,
That the mason work upon the work day,
As truly as he can or may,

To deserve his hire for the holy-day,
And truly to labour on his deed,
Well deserve to have his reward.

Third point

The third point must be severely,
With the 'prentice know it well,
His master's counsel he keep and close,
And his fellows by his good purpose;
The privities of the chamber tell he no man,
Nor in the lodge whatsoever they do;
Whatsoever thou hearest or seest them do,
Tell it no man wheresoever you go;
The counsel of hall, and even of bower,

Keep it well to great honour,
Lest it would turn thyself to blame,
And bring the craft into great shame.

52

Fourth point

The fourth point teacheth us also,
That no man to his craft be false;
Error he shall maintain none
Against the craft, but let it go;
Nor no prejudice he shall no do
To his master, nor his fellow also;
And though the 'prentice be under awe,
Yet he would have the same law.

Fifth point

The fifth point is without doubt,
That when the mason taketh his pay
Of the master, ordained to him,
Full meekly taken so must it be;
Yet must the master by good reason,
Warn him lawfully before noon,
If he will not occupy him no more,
As he hath done there before;
Against this order he may no strive,
If he think well for to thrive.

Sixth point

The sixth point is full given to know,
Both to high and even low,

For such case it might befall;
Among the masons some or all,
Through envy or deadly hate,
Oft ariseth full great debate.
Then ought the mason if that he may,
Put them both under a day;
But love day yet shall they make none,
Till that the work-day you must well take
Leisure enough love day to make,
Hinder their work for such a fray;
To such end then that you them draw.

That they stand well in God's law.

Seventh point

The seventh point he may well mean,
Of well long life that God us lend,
As it descrieth well openly,
Thou shalt not by thy master's wife lie,
Nor by thy fellows', in no manner wise,
Lest the craft would thee despise;
Nor by thy fellows' concubine,
No more thou wouldst he did by thine.
The pain thereof let it be sure,
That he be 'prentice full seven year,
If he forfeit in any of them
So chastised then must he be;
Full much care might there begin,
For such a foul deadly sin.

Eighth point

The eighth point, he may be sure,
If thou hast taken any cure,
Under thy master thou be true,
For that point thou shalt never rue;
A true mediator thou must needs be
To thy master, and thy fellows free;
Do truly all that thou might,
To both parties, and that is good right.

Ninth point

The ninth point we shall him call,
That he be steward of our hall,
If that you be in chamber together,
Each one serve other with mild cheer;
Gentle fellows, you must it know,
For to be stewards all in turn,
Week after week without doubt,
Stewards to be so all in turn about,
Amiably to serve each one other,
As though they were sister and brother;
There shall never one another cost
Free himself to no advantage,
But every man shall be equally free

In that cost, so must it be;
Look that thou pay well every man always,
That thou hast bought any victuals eaten,
That no craving be made to thee,
Nor to thy fellows in no degree,
To man or to woman, whoever he be,
Pay them well and truly, for that will we;
Thereof on thy fellow true record thou take,
For that good pay as thou dost make,
Lest it would thy fellow shame,
And bring thyself into great blame.
Yet good accounts he must make

Of such goods as he hath taken,
Of thy fellows' goods that thou hast spent,
Where and how and to what end;
Such accounts thou must come to,
When thy fellows wish that thou do.

Tenth point

The tenth point presenteth well good life,
To live without care and strife;
For if the mason live amiss,
And in his work be false I know,

And through such a false excuse
May slander his fellows without reason,
Through false slander of such fame

May make the craft acquire blame.
If he do the craft such villainy,
Do him no favour then securely,
Nor maintain not him in wicked life,
Lest it would turn to care and strife;
But yet him you shall not delay,
Unless that you shall him constrain,
For to appear wheresoever you will,
Where that you will, loud, or still;
To the next assembly you him call,
To appear before his fellows all,
And unless he will before them appear,

The craft he must need forswear;
He shall then be punished after the law
That was founded by old day.

Eleventh point

The eleventh point is of good discretion,
As you must know by good reason;
A mason, if he this craft well know,
That seeth his fellow hew on a stone,
And is in point to spoil that stone,
Amend it soon if that thou can,
And teach him then it to amend,
That the lords' work be not spoiled,
And teach him easily it to amend,

With fair words, that God thee hath lent;
For his sake that sit above,
With sweet words nourish his love.

Twelfth point

The twelfth point is of great royalty,
There as the assembly held shall be,
There shall be masters and fellows also,
And other great lords many more;
There shall be the sheriff of that country,
And also the mayor of that city,
Knights and squires there shall be,

And also aldermen, as you shall see;
Such ordinance as thy make there,

They shall maintain it all together
Against that man, whatsoever he be,
That belongeth to the craft both fair and free.
If he any strife against them make,
Into their custody he shall be taken.

Thirteenth point

The thirteenth point is to us full lief,
He shall swear never to be no thief,
Nor succor him in his false craft,
For no good that he hath bereft,
And thou must it know or sin,
Neither for his good, nor for his kin.

Fourteenth point

The fourteenth point is full good law
To him that would be under awe;
A good true oath he must there swear
To his master and his fellows that be there;
He must be steadfast be and true also
To all this ordinance, wheresoever he go,
And to his liege lord the king,
To be true to him over all thing.
And all these points here before
To them thou must need be sworn,
And all shall swear the same oath
Of the masons, be they lief be they loath.
To all these points here before,

That hath been ordained by full good lore.
And they shall enquire every man
Of his party, as well as he can,
If any man may be found guilty
In any of these points specially;
And who he be, let him be sought,
And to the assembly let him be brought.

Fifteen point

The fifteenth point is full good lore,
For them that shall be there sworn,
Such ordinance at the assembly was laid
Of great lords and masters before said;
For the same that be disobedient, I know,

Against the ordinance that there is,
Of these articles that were moved there,
Of great lords and masons all together,
And if they be proved openly
Before that assembly, by and by,
And for their guilt's no amends will make,
Then must they need the craft forsake;
And no masons craft they shall refuse,
And swear it never more to use.
But if that they will amends make,
Again to the craft they shall never take;
And if that they will no do so,
The sheriff shall come them soon to,

And put their bodies in deep prison,
For the trespass that they have done,
And take their goods and their cattle
Into the king's hand, every part,
And let them dwell there full still,
Till it be our liege king's will.

Another ordinance of the art of geometry

They ordained there an assembly to be hold,
Every year, wheresoever they would,
To amend the defaults, if any were found
Among the craft within the land;
Each year or third year it should be held,

In every place wheresoever they would;
Time and place must be ordained also,
In what place they should assemble to,
All the men of craft there they must be,
And other great lords, as you must see,
To mend the faults the he there spoken,
If that any of them be then broken.
There they shall be all sworn,
That belongeth to this craft's lore,
To keep their statutes every one
That were ordained by King Althelstan;
These statutes that I have here found

I ordain they be held through my land,
For the worship of my royalty,
That I have by my dignity.
Also at every assembly that you hold,
That you come to your liege king bold,
Beseeching him of his grace,
To stand with you in every place,
To confirm the statutes of King Athelstan,
That he ordained to this craft by good reason.

The art of the four crowned ones

Pray we now to God almighty,
And to his mother Mary bright,

That we may keep these articles here,
And these points well all together,
As did these holy martyrs four,
That in this craft were of great honour;
They were as good masons as on earth shall go,
Gravers and image-makers they were also.
For they were workmen of the best,
The emperor had to them great liking;
He willed of them an image to make
That might be worshiped for his sake;
Such monuments he had in his day,
To turn the people from Christ's law.

But they were steadfast in Christ's law,
And to their craft without doubt;
They loved well God and all his lore,
And were in his service ever more.
True men they were in that day,
And lived well in God's law;
They thought no monuments for to make,
For no good that they might take,
To believe on that monument for their God,
They would not do so, though he was furious;
For they would not forsake their true faith,

And believe on his false law,
The emperor let take them soon anon,
And put them in a deep prison;
The more sorely he punished them in that place,
The more joy was to them of Christ's grace,
Then when he saw no other one,
To death he let them then go;
By the book he might it show
In legend of holy ones,
The names of the four-crowned ones.

Their feast will be without doubt,
After Hallow-e'en eighth day.
You may hear as I do read,
That many years after, for great dread
That Noah's flood was all run,
The tower of Babylon was begun,
As plain work of lime and stone,
As any man should look upon;
So long and broad it was begun,
Seven miles the height shadoweth the sun.
King Nebuchadnezzar let it make
To great strength for man's sake,
Though such a flood again should come,
Over the work it should not take;
For they had so high pride, with strong boast
All that work therefore was lost;
An angel smote them so with divers speech,
That never one knew what the other should tell.

Many years after, the good clerk Euclid
Taught the craft of geometry full wonder wide,
So he did that other time also,
Of divers crafts many more.
Through high grace of Christ in heaven,
He commenced in the sciences seven;

Grammar is the first science I know,
Dialect the second, so I have I bliss,
Rhetoric the third without doubt,
Music is the fourth, as I you say,

Astronomy is the fifth, by my snout,
Arithmetic the sixth, without doubt,
Geometry the seventh maketh an end,
For he is both meek and courteous,
Grammar forsooth is the root,
Whoever will learn on the book;
But art passeth in his degree,
As the fruit doth the root of the tree;

Rhetoric measureth with ornate speech among,
And music it is a sweet song;
Astronomy numbereth, my dear brother,
Arithmetic sheweth one thing that is another,
Geometry the seventh science it is,
That can separate falsehood from truth, I know
These be the sciences seven,
Who useth them well he may have heaven.
Now dear children by your wit
Pride and covetousness that you leave it,

And taketh heed to good discretion,
And to good nurture, wheresoever you come.
Now I pray you take good heed,

For this you must know needs,
But much more you must know,
Than you find here written.
If thee fail thereto wit,
Pray to God to send thee it;
For Christ himself, he teacheth us
That holy church is God's house,
That is made for nothing else
But for to pray in, as the book tells us;
There the people shall gather in,
To pray and weep for their sin.
Look thou come not to church late,
For to speak harlotry by the gate;

Then to church when thou dost fare,
Have in thy mind ever more
To worship thy lord God both day and night,
With all thy wits and even thy might.
To the church door when thou dost come
Of that holy water there some thou take,
For every drop thou feelest there
Quencheth a venial sin, be thou sure.
But first thou must do down thy hood,
For his love that died on the rood.
Into the church when thou dost go,
Pull up thy heart to Christ, anon;

Upon the rood thou look up then,
And kneel down fair upon thy knees,
Then pray to him so here to work,
After the law of holy church,

For to keep the commandments ten,
That God gave to all men;
And pray to him with mild voice
To keep thee from the sins seven,
That thou here may, in this life,
Keep thee well from care and strife;
Furthermore he grant thee grace,
In heaven's bliss to have a place.

In holy church leave trifling words
Of lewd speech and foul jests,
And put away all vanity,
And say thy pater noster and thine ave;
Look also that thou make no noise,
But always to be in thy prayer;
If thou wilt not thyself pray,
Hinder no other man by no way.
In that place neither sit nor stand,
But kneel fair down on the ground,
And when the Gospel me read shall,

Fairly thou stand up from the wall,
And bless the fare if that thou can,
When gloria tibi is begun;
And when the gospel is done,
Again thou might kneel down,

On both knees down thou fall,
For his love that bought us all;
And when thou hearest the bell ring
To that holy sacrament,
Kneel you must both young and old,
And both your hands fair uphold,
And say then in this manner,

Fair and soft without noise;
"Jesu Lord welcome thou be,
In form of bread as I thee see,
Now Jesu for thine holy name,
Shield me from sin and shame;
Shrift and Eucharist thou grand me both,
Ere that I shall hence go,
And very contrition for my sin,
That I never, Lord, die therein;
And as thou were of maid born,
Suffer me never to be lost;
But when I shall hence wend,

Grant me the bliss without end;
Amen! Amen! so mote it be!
Now sweet lady pray for me."
Thus thou might say, or some other thing,
When thou kneelest at the sacrament.
For covetousness after good, spare thou not
To worship him that all hath wrought;

For glad may a man that day be,
That once in the day may him see;

It is so much worth, without doubt,
The virtue thereof no man tell may;
But so much good doth that sight,

That Saint Austin telleth full right,
That day thou seest God's body,
Thou shalt have these full securely:-
Meet and drink at thy need,
None that day shalt thou lack;
Idle oaths and words both,
God forgiveth thee also;
Sudden death that same day
Thee dare not dread by no way;
Also that day, I thee plight,
Thou shalt not lose thy eye sight;
And each foot that thou goest then,

That holy sight for to see,
They shall be told to stand instead,
When thou hast thereto great need;
That messenger the angel Gabriel,
Will keep them to thee full well.
From this matter now I may pass,
To tell more benefits of the mass:
To church come yet, if thou may,
And hear the mass each day;
If thou may not come to church,
Where that ever thou dost work,
When thou hearest the mass toll,

Pray to God with heart still,
To give thy part of that service,
That in church there done is.
Furthermore yet, I will you preach
To your fellows, it for to teach,
When thou comest before a lord,
In hall, in bower, or at the board,
Hood or cap that thou off do,
Ere thou come him entirely to;
Twice or thrice, without doubt,
To that lord thou must bow;
With thy right knee let it be done,

Thine own worship thou save so.
Hold off thy cap and hood also,
Till thou have leave it on to put.
All the time thou speakest with him,
Fair and amiably hold up thy chin;
So after the nurture of the book,
In his face kindly thou look.
Foot and hand thou keep full still,
For clawing and tripping, is skill;
From spitting and sniffling keep thee also,
By private expulsion let it go,
And if that thou be wise and discrete,

Thou has great need to govern thee well.
Into the hall when thou dost wend,
Amongst the gentles, good and courteous,
Presume not too high for nothing,
For thine high blood, nor thy cunning,

Neither to sit nor to lean,
That is nurture good and clean.
Let not thy countenance therefor abate,
Forsooth good nurture will save thy state.
Father and mother, whatsoever they be,
Well is the child that well may thee,
In hall, in chamber, where thou dost go;

Good manners make a man.
To the next degree look wisely,
To do them reverence by and by;
Do them yet no reverence all in turn,
Unless that thou do them know.
To the meat when thou art set,
Fair and honestly thou eat it;
First look that thine hands be clean,
And that thy knife be sharp and keen,
And cut thy bread all at thy meat,
Right as it may be there eaten,
If thou sit by a worthier man,

Then thy self thou art one,
Suffer him first to touch the meat,
Ere thyself to it reach.
To the fairest morsel thou might not strike,
Though that thou do it well like;
Keep thine hands fair and well,
From foul smudging of thy towel;
Thereon thou shalt not thy nose blow,
Nor at the meat thy tooth thou pick;
Too deep in cup thou might not sink,

Though thou have good will to drink,
Lest thine eyes would water thereby—

Then were it no courtesy.
Look in thy mouth there be no meat,
When thou begins to drink or speak.
When thou seest any man drinking,
That taketh heed to thy speech,
Soon anaon thou cease thy tale,
Whether he drink wine or ale,
Look also thou scorn no man,
In what degree thou seest him gone;
Nor thou shalt no man deprave,
If thou wilt thy worship save;
For such word might there outburst.

That might make thee sit in evil rest.
Close thy hand in thy fist,
And keep thee well from "had I known."
Hold thy tongue and spend thy sight;
Laugh thou not with no great cry,
Nor make no lewd sport and ribaldry.
Play thou not but with thy peers,
Nor tell thou not all that thou hears;
Discover thou not thine own deed,
For no mirth, nor for no reward;
With fair speech thou might have thy will,
With it thou might thy self spoil.

When thou meetest a worthy man,
Cap and hood thou hold not on;

In church, in market, or in the gate,
Do him reverance after his state.
If thou goest with a worthier man
Then thyself thou art one,
Let thy foremost shoulder follow his back,
For that is nurture without lack;

When he doth speak, hold thee still,
When he hath done, say for thy will,
In thy speech that thou be discreet,
And what thou sayest consider thee well;
But deprive thou not him his tale,
Neither at the wine nor at the ale.
Christ then of his high grace,
Save you both wit and space,
Well this book to know and read,
Heaven to have for your reward.
Amen! Amen! so mote it be!
So say we all for charity.

www.ingramcontent.com/pod-product-compliance
Lightning Source LLC
LaVergne TN
LVHW041634070426
835507LV00008B/618